Mastering Photo Editing: A Beginner's Guide to Adobe Lightroom

Table of Contents

Chapter 1: Introducing Adobe Lightroom

Welcome to the world of Adobe Lightroom! In this chapter, we'll take you through the basics of Lightroom, from installation to navigating the interface. By the end of this tutorial, you'll be ready to start importing and organizing your photos in Lightroom. Let's get started!

Step 1: Installing Adobe Lightroom

Go to the Adobe website (www.adobe.com) and sign in with your Adobe ID or create a new account if you don't have one.

Once you're logged in, navigate to the "Creative Cloud" section and click on "Apps."

Scroll down to find "Adobe Lightroom" and click on "Download" or "Install" to get the latest version.

Follow the installation instructions for your operating system (Windows or macOS).

Step 2: Opening Adobe Lightroom

Launch Adobe Lightroom from your computer's application list or desktop shortcut.

If you're opening Lightroom for the first time, you'll be prompted to sign in with your Adobe ID.

Once signed in, you'll see the Lightroom home screen, which provides access to the Library, Develop, Map, Book, Slideshow, Print, and Web modules.

Step 3: Navigating the Lightroom Interface

The Library module is where you'll manage and organize your photos. Click on "Library" at the top to enter this mode.

On the left panel, you'll find various sections such as Catalog, Folders, Collections, and more. These will help you organize your photo library efficiently.

The center panel will display the thumbnails of your imported images. You can use the Filmstrip at the bottom to browse through them.

The right panel contains the metadata, keywords, and other information about the selected image.

To switch to the Develop module, click on "Develop" at the top. This is where you'll make adjustments to your photos to enhance their look.

Step 4: Importing Photos into Lightroom

In the Library module, click on the "Import" button at the bottom-left corner of the screen.

A dialog box will appear, showing your computer's files and folders. Navigate to the location where your photos are stored.

Select the images you want to import by clicking on them. You can also choose to import all photos in a folder.

In the right panel, you can add keywords, apply presets, and choose the destination folder for the imported photos.

Once you're satisfied with the import settings, click the "Import" button at the bottom-right corner of the dialog box.

Congratulations! You've completed the first chapter of our Adobe Lightroom tutorial. Now you know how to install Lightroom, navigate the interface, and import your photos. In the next chapter, we'll dive into the Library module, where you'll learn how to organize and manage your photo library effectively. Happy editing!

Chapter 2: Importing Photos

In the previous chapter, you learned how to install Adobe Lightroom and navigate its interface. Now, let's dive into the Library module, where you'll learn how to import, organize, and manage your photos efficiently. By the end of this tutorial, you'll be a pro at importing photos into Lightroom. Let's get started!

Step 1: Accessing the Library Module

Open Adobe Lightroom if you haven't already done so.

Click on the "Library" module at the top of the screen to enter the Library mode.

Step 2: Creating a New Catalog (Optional)

When you first launch Lightroom, you'll be asked to create a new catalog or choose an existing one. A catalog is like a database that stores information about your photos.

If you're starting from scratch, create a new catalog by clicking "Create New" and giving it a name and location. This step is optional, and you can work with the default catalog as well.

Step 3: Connecting Your Camera or Memory Card (Optional)

If you're using a camera or memory card, you can connect it to your computer now.

Lightroom will detect the connected device and display it in the left panel under "Devices."

Step 4: Importing Photos from Your Computer

Click on "File" in the top menu and select "Import Photos and Videos" or simply press "Ctrl + Shift + I" (Windows) or "Cmd + Shift + I" (macOS).

The import dialog box will appear, displaying your computer's files and folders.

Navigate to the folder containing the photos you want to import. You can use the left panel to browse through your computer's directory structure.

Click on the images you want to import. Selected photos will have a checkmark on their thumbnails.

If you want to import all photos in a folder, click on the folder name, and all photos will be selected.

In the right panel, you'll see various import options:

File Handling: Choose how Lightroom handles your files, including file renaming and file handling.

File Renaming: Rename your photos upon import using custom naming conventions.

Apply During Import: Apply metadata presets, keywords, and develop settings during import.

Destination: Choose where you want to store the imported photos in your Lightroom catalog.

Step 5: Reviewing and Importing Photos

Take a moment to review the import settings to ensure everything is as you want it.

Click the "Import" button at the bottom-right corner of the import dialog box to start the import process.

Step 6: Viewing Imported Photos

After the import is complete, you'll see your imported photos in the center panel of the Library module.

Use the Filmstrip at the bottom to scroll through the imported images.

Congratulations! You've learned how to import photos into Adobe Lightroom efficiently. In the next chapter, we'll explore the Library module further, discussing how to organize and manage your photo library effectively using folders, collections, and keywords. Keep up the good work!

Chapter 3: Understanding the Library Module

In the previous chapter, you mastered the art of importing photos into Adobe Lightroom. Now, let's delve deeper into the Library module, where you'll learn how to organize and manage your photo library effectively. By the end of this tutorial, you'll be a pro at using folders, collections, and keywords to keep your photos in order. Let's get started!

Step 1: Reviewing the Library Module Interface

Open Adobe Lightroom and click on the "Library" module at the top of the screen to enter the Library mode.

Familiarize yourself with the interface:

The left panel contains several sections, such as Catalog, Folders, Collections, and more.

The center panel displays the thumbnails of your imported images.

The right panel provides information and settings related to the selected image.

Step 2: Organizing with Folders

In the left panel, under "Folders," you'll see a list of all the folders where your photos are stored.

To create a new folder, right-click on "Folders" and select "Add Folder" or click on the "+" icon at the top-right corner of the "Folders" section.

Name the new folder and choose its location on your computer.

Drag and drop photos from the center panel into the newly created folder to organize them.

Step 3: Working with Collections

Collections are virtual groups of images that allow you to organize photos without physically moving them into different folders.

To create a new collection, click on the "+" icon next to "Collections" in the left panel and choose "Create Collection."

Name the collection and click "Create."

To add photos to the collection, drag and drop images from the center panel into the collection name in the left panel.

Step 4: Utilizing Keywords

Keywords are essential for organizing and finding photos quickly.

In the right panel, under the "Keywording" section, click on the empty field and start typing keywords related to the selected photo.

Separate multiple keywords with commas, and press Enter after each keyword.

You can add keywords to multiple images simultaneously by selecting them in the center panel and adding the keywords in the right panel.

Step 5: Filtering and Sorting

Use the Filter Bar at the top of the center panel to quickly find specific photos based on attributes like flags, star ratings, keywords, and more.

Click on the attribute you want to filter by and select the desired criteria from the dropdown menu.

To sort your photos, click on the column headers in the center panel, such as "Capture Time" or "File Name."

Step 6: Flags, Star Ratings, and Color Labels

Use flags to mark photos as "Picked" (flagged) or "Rejected" during the culling process. Press "P" to pick and "X" to reject.

Assign star ratings to photos to indicate their quality or importance. Press 1 to 5 on your keyboard to assign stars.

Color labels can be used for additional categorization. Press the corresponding number keys (6 to 9) to assign colors.

Congratulations! You've now learned how to organize and manage your photo library in Adobe Lightroom using folders, collections, keywords, and filters. In the next chapter, we'll dive into the art of basic photo editing using Lightroom's Develop module. Keep up the great work on your photo editing journey!

Chapter 4: Basic Photo Editing in Lightroom's Develop Module

In the previous chapter, you learned how to organize and manage your photo library effectively using Adobe Lightroom's Library module. Now, it's time to enhance the visual appeal of your photos using the powerful editing tools in the Develop module. By the end of this tutorial, you'll be confident in making basic adjustments to your images. Let's get started!

Step 1: Accessing the Develop Module

Open Adobe Lightroom if it's not already running.

Click on the "Develop" module at the top of the screen to enter the Develop mode.

Step 2: Understanding the Develop Module Interface

Familiarize yourself with the interface:

The left panel contains various editing sections like "Basic," "Tone Curve," "HSL/Color," and more.

The center panel displays your selected photo, and any adjustments you make will be visible here.

The right panel provides additional settings and options for fine-tuning your edits.

Step 3: Making Basic Adjustments

In the "Basic" section of the left panel, you'll find the fundamental adjustments for your photo:

Exposure: Adjust the overall brightness of the image.

Contrast: Increase or decrease the difference between light and dark areas.

Highlights and Shadows: Fine-tune the bright and dark regions of your photo.

Whites and Blacks: Adjust the brightest and darkest points of your image.

Step 4: White Balance and Color Adjustments

In the "Basic" section, you'll also find the "White Balance" controls:

Temperature: Adjust the warmth or coolness of your image.

Tint: Fine-tune the green or magenta tint in your photo.

The "HSL/Color" section allows you to adjust specific colors in your image:

Hue: Change the color tone of a specific range of colors.

Saturation: Increase or decrease the intensity of colors.

Luminance: Adjust the brightness of specific colors.

Step 5: Sharpening and Noise Reduction

The "Detail" section in the right panel provides options for sharpening and reducing noise in your image:

Amount: Increase the sharpness to enhance details.

Radius: Adjust the size of the sharpening area.

Detail and Masking: Fine-tune the sharpening effect.

Noise Reduction: Reduce digital noise in high ISO images.

Step 6: Before and After View

To see the before and after view of your edits, press the backslash key "" on your keyboard.

This will toggle between the original and edited versions of your photo.

Step 7: Syncing and Copying Edits (Optional)

If you want to apply the same edits to multiple photos, select the edited photo and click on "Sync..." at the bottom of the right panel.

Check the settings you want to synchronize and click "Synchronize."

You can also copy edits from one photo and apply them to another by selecting the edited photo and clicking on "Copy..." at the bottom of the right panel. Then, select the target photo and click "Paste."

Congratulations! You've learned the basics of photo editing in Adobe Lightroom's Develop module. Play around with these adjustments to see how they transform your images. In the next chapter, we'll explore advanced editing techniques, such as local adjustments and graduated filters. Keep practicing and improving your photo editing skills!

Chapter 5: Advanced Editing Techniques in Lightroom's Develop Module

In the previous chapter, you learned the basics of photo editing in Adobe Lightroom's Develop module. Now, it's time to take your editing skills to the next level with advanced techniques. In this tutorial, you'll discover how to make precise adjustments using local adjustments and graduated filters. By the end of this chapter, you'll be able to create stunning images with expert-level editing finesse. Let's dive in!

Step 1: Using the Adjustment Brush

In the "Develop" module, find the "Adjustment Brush" tool in the right panel or press "K" on your keyboard to activate it.

The brush allows you to make targeted adjustments to specific areas of your photo.

Adjust the brush settings in the right panel:

Size: Change the brush size using the slider or bracket keys "[" and "]".

Feather: Control the softness of the brush edges.

Flow: Set the intensity of the adjustments applied by the brush.

Density: Adjust the strength of the brush's effect.

Step 2: Making Local Adjustments

With the Adjustment Brush active, select the settings you want to modify, such as exposure, contrast, clarity, or saturation.

Paint over the area you wish to adjust using the brush. The adjustment will only apply to the painted region.

To view the masked areas, press the "O" key on your keyboard to enable the mask overlay. This will show where the adjustment is being applied.

Step 3: Using the Graduated Filter

Locate the "Graduated Filter" tool in the right panel or press "M" on your keyboard to activate it.

The graduated filter applies adjustments gradually, creating a smooth transition between the affected and unaffected areas.

Adjust the filter settings in the right panel:

Exposure, contrast, highlights, shadows, etc., can be modified just like in the Adjustment Brush.

Click and drag the filter overlay to define the direction and angle of the gradient.

Step 4: Applying Local Adjustments to Multiple Areas

You can add multiple adjustments using both the Adjustment Brush and Graduated Filter.

Click the "+" icon in the right panel to create a new adjustment.

Make additional adjustments by painting with the brush or drawing additional graduated filters.

Step 5: Erasing and Fine-Tuning Local Adjustments

To erase parts of a local adjustment, select the "Eraser" tool (found within the Adjustment Brush or Graduated Filter).

Paint over the areas where you want to remove the effect. You can adjust the size and feather of the eraser in the right panel.

To fine-tune any local adjustment, use the sliders in the right panel to modify the strength of the effect or double-click the pin to re-open the adjustment settings.

Step 6: Syncing and Copying Local Adjustments (Optional)

If you've applied similar local adjustments to multiple photos, select the edited photo with the adjustments you want to sync.

Click on "Sync..." at the bottom of the right panel, check the desired settings, and click "Synchronize" to apply those adjustments to other selected photos.

You can also copy local adjustments from one photo and paste them onto another using the "Copy..." and "Paste" options.

Congratulations! You've now mastered advanced editing techniques in Adobe Lightroom's Develop module. Local adjustments and graduated filters allow you to precisely control the look and feel of your images, giving them a professional touch. In the next chapter, we'll explore creative editing with presets, allowing you to apply artistic effects to your photos with just a few clicks. Keep honing your editing skills and unlocking your creativity!

Chapter 6: Creative Editing with Presets in Adobe Lightroom

In the previous chapter, you learned advanced editing techniques in Adobe Lightroom's Develop module. Now, let's explore the world of creative editing with presets. Presets are pre-defined settings that allow you to apply artistic effects and styles to your photos quickly and easily. In this tutorial, you'll discover how to use presets and even create your own. Let's dive in and unleash your creativity!

Step 1: Accessing the Presets Panel

In the "Develop" module, find the "Presets" panel on the left side of the screen.

Click the triangle icon to expand the panel and reveal the list of available presets.

Step 2: Applying Presets to Your Photos

Browse through the preset categories to find the style you want to apply. Categories may include "Color," "Black & White," "Portrait," "Landscape," and more.

Step 6: Syncing and Copying Local Adjustments (Optional)

If you've applied similar local adjustments to multiple photos, select the edited photo with the adjustments you want to sync.

Click on "Sync..." at the bottom of the right panel, check the desired settings, and click "Synchronize" to apply those adjustments to other selected photos.

You can also copy local adjustments from one photo and paste them onto another using the "Copy..." and "Paste" options.

Congratulations! You've now mastered advanced editing techniques in Adobe Lightroom's Develop module. Local adjustments and graduated filters allow you to precisely control the look and feel of your images, giving them a professional touch. In the next chapter, we'll explore creative editing with presets, allowing you to apply artistic effects to your photos with just a few clicks. Keep honing your editing skills and unlocking your creativity!

Chapter 6: Creative Editing with Presets in Adobe Lightroom

In the previous chapter, you learned advanced editing techniques in Adobe Lightroom's Develop module. Now, let's explore the world of creative editing with presets. Presets are pre-defined settings that allow you to apply artistic effects and styles to your photos quickly and easily. In this tutorial, you'll discover how to use presets and even create your own. Let's dive in and unleash your creativity!

Step 1: Accessing the Presets Panel

In the "Develop" module, find the "Presets" panel on the left side of the screen.

Click the triangle icon to expand the panel and reveal the list of available presets.

Step 2: Applying Presets to Your Photos

Browse through the preset categories to find the style you want to apply. Categories may include "Color," "Black & White," "Portrait," "Landscape," and more.

Click on a preset name to apply it to your selected photo. The changes will be instantly visible in the center panel.

Step 3: Using the Navigator Presets (Optional)

Lightroom also offers "Navigator Presets" that allow you to preview the look of a preset before applying it fully.

Hover over a preset name, and you'll see a small preview of the effect in the Navigator window.

Click on the preview to apply the effect temporarily. This lets you see how the preset affects your photo without committing to it.

Step 4: Fine-Tuning Preset Effects

After applying a preset, you can adjust its intensity using the "Amount" slider in the "Presets" panel.

Drag the slider left to reduce the effect or right to increase it until you achieve your desired look.

Step 5: Creating Your Own Presets

To create a custom preset from your edited photo, make sure all the desired adjustments are applied to the image.

In the left panel, find the "Presets" panel and click on the "+" icon to create a new preset.

Name your preset and choose the settings you want to include in it. You can select everything or just specific adjustments like exposure, contrast, color, etc.

Click "Create" to save your custom preset.

Step 6: Managing Presets

Lightroom allows you to organize your presets for easy access.

In the "Presets" panel, right-click on a preset to create a new folder, rename it, or delete it.

You can also organize presets into folders by dragging and dropping them.

Step 7: Importing and Exporting Presets (Optional)

If you have additional presets you want to use, you can import them into Lightroom.

Click on the "+" icon in the "Presets" panel and choose "Import Presets."

Locate the preset files on your computer and click "Import."

To share your custom presets with others, right-click on the preset and choose "Export."

Step 8: Resetting Presets

To remove a preset from a photo and return to its original state, click "Reset" at the bottom of the "Develop" panel.

Congratulations! You've now unlocked the power of creative editing with presets in Adobe Lightroom. Experiment with different presets and create your own unique styles. In the next chapter, we'll delve into the world of working with RAW files, allowing you to maximize the potential of your images. Keep up the great work and continue exploring your creative vision!

Chapter 7: Working with RAW Files in Adobe Lightroom

In the previous chapter, you explored the creative world of presets in Adobe Lightroom. Now, let's dive into the realm of RAW files, where you'll discover the benefits of shooting in RAW and learn how to make the most of these high-quality image files in Lightroom. By the end of this tutorial, you'll be equipped to handle RAW files and unleash their full potential. Let's get started!

Step 1: Understanding RAW Files

RAW files are uncompressed and unprocessed image files captured directly by your camera's sensor.

Unlike JPEG files, RAW files retain all the image data, providing greater flexibility for editing without sacrificing image quality.

Step 2: Importing RAW Files into Lightroom

The process of importing RAW files is similar to importing JPEGs or other image formats. Simply follow the steps in Chapter 2: Importing Photos.

Step 3: RAW File Development

After importing a RAW file, enter the "Develop" module to begin editing.

Notice that RAW files open with minimal adjustments applied, giving you a clean slate for editing.

Step 4: Basic Adjustments for RAW Files

RAW files offer greater latitude for exposure adjustments. Use the "Exposure," "Highlights," "Shadows," "Whites," and "Blacks" sliders to fine-tune the exposure without sacrificing details.

Adjust the "White Balance" settings to achieve the desired color temperature and tint.

Take advantage of RAW's dynamic range to recover details from both highlight and shadow areas.

Step 5: Utilizing the Tone Curve for Precise Adjustments

The "Tone Curve" allows you to make targeted adjustments to different tonal ranges in your image.

Use the "Point Curve" or the "Parametric Curve" to fine-tune highlights, lights, darks, and shadows.

The "Tone Curve" provides unparalleled control over your image's tonalities.

Step 6: Detail Enhancements with Sharpening and Noise Reduction

RAW files may benefit from slightly different sharpening and noise reduction settings than other file formats.

Adjust the "Sharpening" settings carefully to enhance details without introducing artifacts.

Use the "Noise Reduction" settings to reduce noise while preserving image details.

Step 7: Utilizing Lens Corrections for RAW Files

RAW files may contain lens distortions and chromatic aberrations. Lightroom offers automatic lens corrections for many lenses.

In the "Lens Corrections" panel, check the "Enable Profile Corrections" box to apply automatic corrections based on your lens and camera combination.

Step 8: Embracing Non-Destructive Editing with RAW Files

Remember that Lightroom's editing process is non-destructive, meaning your original RAW file remains untouched.

Edits are stored as metadata, and you can revert to the original at any time.

Step 9: Exporting RAW Files

When you're satisfied with your edits, export your RAW files to JPEG or other formats for sharing or printing.

Go to the "File" menu, select "Export," and choose your preferred settings.

Step 10: Backing Up Your RAW Files

RAW files are valuable digital negatives, so it's crucial to back them up regularly to prevent data loss.

Create redundant backups on external hard drives or cloud storage for added security.

Congratulations! You've mastered working with RAW files in Adobe Lightroom. RAW formats offer unparalleled flexibility and quality, making them ideal for professional and advanced photographers. In the next chapter, we'll delve into managing noise and sharpening in your images to achieve the best results. Keep up the excellent work on your photo editing journey!

Chapter 8: Managing Noise and Sharpening in Adobe Lightroom

In the previous chapter, you learned the art of working with RAW files in Adobe Lightroom. Now, let's explore the essential techniques of managing noise and sharpening to enhance the clarity and quality of your images. In this tutorial, you'll discover how to reduce noise in high ISO images and apply targeted sharpening for crisp, detailed photos. Let's get started on perfecting your images!

Step 1: Understanding Noise in Images

Noise is the random variation of brightness or color that can appear in photos, particularly in low-light or high ISO situations.

Noise can affect the overall quality and sharpness of your images.

Step 2: Reducing Noise in Adobe Lightroom

Enter the "Develop" module and find the "Detail" panel in the right panel.

Locate the "Noise Reduction" section and adjust the "Luminance" and "Color" sliders to reduce noise.

Step 3: Adjusting Luminance Noise Reduction

Slide the "Luminance" slider to the right to reduce luminance noise (grainy appearance).

Be cautious not to overdo it, as excessive noise reduction can soften the image.

Step 4: Managing Color Noise Reduction

Use the "Color" slider to reduce color noise in your images.

Be mindful of balancing color noise reduction to maintain natural colors and avoid color artifacts.

Step 5: Applying Targeted Sharpening

In the same "Detail" panel, you'll find the "Sharpening" section.

Adjust the "Amount" slider to increase or decrease overall sharpening.

Use the "Radius" slider to control the area of sharpening. Lower values sharpen finer details, while higher values sharpen broader areas.

The "Detail" slider enhances edge details, while the "Masking" slider limits sharpening to areas with more contrast.

Step 6: Previewing Noise Reduction and Sharpening

To view the effect of noise reduction and sharpening, zoom in on your image using the Navigator panel or by pressing "Z" and clicking on the area you want to inspect.

Press the "P" key to toggle the preview on and off, allowing you to see the changes you've made.

Step 7: Applying Noise Reduction and Sharpening Locally

If specific areas of your image require different noise reduction or sharpening settings, consider using the Adjustment Brush or Graduated Filter.

Use the Adjustment Brush with negative clarity and sharpness settings to soften skin or create a smooth effect selectively.

Apply sharpness with the Adjustment Brush or Graduated Filter to specific elements in your image that need extra emphasis.

Step 8: Striking the Right Balance

Finding the perfect balance of noise reduction and sharpening can vary depending on the image and its intended use.

Aim for a balance that reduces noise while preserving image details, resulting in a clear and natural-looking photo.

Step 9: Preserving Image Quality

Keep in mind that noise reduction and sharpening are global adjustments that can affect your entire image.

Always use non-destructive editing techniques in Lightroom to preserve your original RAW file and make adjustments as needed.

Congratulations! You've now mastered the art of managing noise and sharpening in Adobe Lightroom. These techniques will help you achieve clear, high-quality images that stand out. In the next chapter, we'll explore correcting lens distortions and perspective issues to ensure your photos are distortion-free. Keep up the excellent work on your photo editing journey!

Chapter 9: Correcting Lens Distortions and Perspective Issues in Adobe Lightroom

In the previous chapter, you learned how to manage noise and sharpen your images in Adobe Lightroom. Now, let's tackle another essential aspect of photo editing—correcting lens distortions and perspective issues. In this tutorial, you'll discover how to identify and fix common lens distortions and achieve distortion-free images with proper perspective adjustments. Let's get started on perfecting your photos!

Step 1: Identifying Lens Distortions

Lens distortions can occur in photos due to various factors, such as the lens's optical characteristics.

Common lens distortions include barrel distortion (outward bulging), pincushion distortion (inward pinching), and vignetting (darkening around the corners).

Step 2: Applying Lens Corrections in Adobe Lightroom

Enter the "Develop" module and find the "Lens Corrections" panel in the right panel.

In the "Basic" tab, check the "Enable Profile Corrections" box to apply automatic lens corrections based on your camera and lens combination.

Lightroom will recognize your lens and apply corrections to fix distortions and vignetting.

Step 3: Fine-Tuning Lens Corrections (Optional)

In the "Lens Corrections" panel, switch to the "Manual" tab to fine-tune the corrections further.

Adjust the "Distortion" slider to correct barrel or pincushion distortion manually, if necessary.

The "Vignetting" sliders allow you to control the amount of darkening in the corners.

Step 4: Correcting Perspective Issues

Perspective issues can occur when shooting architecture or tall structures, resulting in converging vertical lines.

In the "Transform" panel (located below the "Lens Corrections" panel), you'll find various tools to fix perspective issues.

Step 5: Using the Guided Upright Tool

The Guided Upright Tool is ideal for correcting perspective in specific photos.

Click on the "Guided Upright" icon (the fourth icon from the left) in the "Transform" panel.

Draw two or more guides along vertical or horizontal lines that should be straight in your image.

Lightroom will automatically correct the perspective and straighten the lines.

Step 6: Manual Transform Adjustments

If the Guided Upright Tool doesn't fully correct the perspective, try the manual adjustments in the "Transform" panel.

The "Vertical," "Horizontal," and "Rotate" sliders allow you to fine-tune the perspective correction.

Step 7: Constrain Crop (Optional)

Perspective corrections may result in empty areas around the edges of the image.

To maintain the original image size, check the "Constrain Crop" box in the "Transform" panel. This will crop the image while preserving its proportions.

Step 8: Re-Crop and Reframe (Optional)

After applying perspective corrections, you may need to re-crop and reframe your image.

Use the crop overlay tool (shortcut "R") to adjust the crop and maintain the desired composition.

Step 9: Review and Fine-Tune

Zoom in on your image to check the results of your lens corrections and perspective adjustments.

Make any necessary fine-tuning to achieve the best possible outcome.

Congratulations! You've now mastered correcting lens distortions and perspective issues in Adobe Lightroom. These adjustments ensure your photos are distortion-free and visually appealing. In the next chapter, we'll explore the art of black and white photography and how to create stunning monochrome images in Lightroom. Keep up the excellent work on your photo editing journey!

Chapter 10: Mastering Black and White Photography in Adobe Lightroom

In the previous chapter, you learned how to correct lens distortions and perspective issues in Adobe Lightroom. Now, let's explore the timeless art of black and white photography. In this tutorial, you'll discover how to create stunning monochrome images and evoke emotion through the absence of color. Let's embark on the journey of mastering black and white photography!

Step 1: Converting to Black and White

Enter the "Develop" module and find the "Basic" panel in the right panel.

Locate the "Treatment" dropdown menu and choose "Black & White" to convert your image.

Step 2: Adjusting Black and White Mix

With the image in black and white, you'll see the "Black & White Mix" panel below the "Basic" panel.

Use the sliders to adjust the brightness of specific colors in your black and white image.

Experiment with the sliders to create the desired tonal contrast and mood.

Step 3: Enhancing Tonal Contrast with Curves

The "Tone Curve" panel allows you to fine-tune the tonal contrast in your black and white image.

Create an S-shaped curve by dragging the bottom-left point slightly upward and the top-right point slightly downward.

This enhances the highlights and shadows, adding depth and drama to your monochrome photo.

Step 4: Controlling Luminance with HSL

In the "HSL/Color" panel, switch to the "Black & White" tab.

Use the "Luminance" sliders to control the brightness of individual colors in your black and white image.

Adjusting these sliders can add or reduce the luminance of specific elements, making them stand out or blend harmoniously.

Step 5: Adding Grain (Optional)

For a classic film-like effect, you can add grain to your black and white image.

In the "Effects" panel, find the "Grain" section and adjust the "Amount," "Size," and "Roughness" sliders to add grain texture.

Step 6: Dodging and Burning (Optional)

To enhance the focal points or create a sense of depth, use the "Adjustment Brush" with positive exposure (dodging) or negative exposure (burning).

Paint over the areas you want to lighten or darken, selectively bringing attention to specific elements.

Step 7: Split Toning (Optional)

If you want to add subtle tones to your black and white image, try the "Split Toning" panel.

Select hues for highlights and shadows, and adjust the "Balance" slider to control the balance between the two.

Step 8: Fine-Tuning and Reviewing

Zoom in on your black and white image to review the details and overall look.

Fine-tune any adjustments to achieve the desired artistic effect.

Step 9: Preserving the Color Version (Optional)

If you want to preserve the color version while working in black and white, create a virtual copy of your image.

Right-click on the image in the Filmstrip, choose "Create Virtual Copy," and proceed with the black and white edits.

Step 10: Saving and Exporting

Once you're satisfied with your black and white masterpiece, save your edits by clicking "Done" or "Close" in the "Develop" module.

To export your image, go to the "File" menu, select "Export," and choose your preferred settings for sharing or printing.

Congratulations! You've now mastered black and white photography in Adobe Lightroom. Monochrome images have a unique ability to evoke emotions and highlight the beauty of simplicity. In the next chapter, we'll explore the world of advanced photo retouching, allowing you to polish your portraits and bring out the best in your subjects. Keep up the great work on your photo editing journey!

Chapter 11: Advanced Photo Retouching in Adobe Lightroom

In the previous chapter, you learned the art of black and white photography in Adobe Lightroom. Now, let's take your photo editing skills to the next level with advanced retouching techniques for portraits and other images. In this tutorial, you'll discover how to polish your photos, remove blemishes, and enhance your subjects. Let's delve into the world of advanced photo retouching!

Step 1: Spot Removal Tool

Enter the "Develop" module and find the "Spot Removal" tool in the toolbar, or press "Q" on your keyboard to activate it.

The Spot Removal tool allows you to remove blemishes, dust spots, and unwanted distractions from your image.

Step 2: Removing Blemishes

Zoom in on your photo to focus on the areas that need retouching.

Adjust the size of the Spot Removal tool using the slider or bracket keys "[" and "]".

Click on a blemish or distraction you want to remove, and Lightroom will automatically clone or heal the area.

For more precise control, manually adjust the position of the source area using the drag handle.

Step 3: Softening Skin and Reducing Wrinkles (Optional)

To soften skin or reduce wrinkles, use the Adjustment Brush with negative clarity and sharpness settings.

Paint over the areas you want to soften, and adjust the brush settings for a natural look.

Step 4: Enhancing Eyes

Use the Adjustment Brush to enhance the eyes by increasing clarity and sharpness.

Paint over the irises and adjust the brush settings to make the eyes more captivating.

Step 5: Whitening Teeth (Optional)

For portrait retouching, you can whiten teeth using the Adjustment Brush with increased exposure and reduced saturation.

Paint over the teeth to make them appear brighter.

Step 6: Dodging and Burning

Use the Adjustment Brush with positive exposure (dodging) or negative exposure (burning) to emphasize or darken specific areas.

Dodge areas you want to highlight and burn areas you want to darken.

Step 7: Using the Graduated Filter (Optional)

The Graduated Filter tool can be useful for retouching specific areas with a gradual effect.

Use it to enhance the sky, balance exposure, or add creative vignettes.

Step 8: Portrait Presets (Optional)

To streamline your portrait retouching workflow, consider using portrait-specific presets available in Lightroom.

Browse through the presets in the "Presets" panel to find those that complement your portrait style.

Step 9: Review and Fine-Tuning

Zoom in on your photo to check for any imperfections and ensure a natural look.

Fine-tune your retouching adjustments to achieve the desired result.

Step 10: Saving and Exporting

Once you're satisfied with your retouched image, save your edits by clicking "Done" or "Close" in the "Develop" module.

To export your photo, go to the "File" menu, select "Export," and choose your preferred settings for sharing or printing.

Congratulations! You've now mastered advanced photo retouching in Adobe Lightroom. These techniques will help you bring out the best in your subjects and create stunning, polished portraits. In the next chapter, we'll explore the world of advanced color adjustments, allowing you to achieve your desired artistic vision. Keep up the great work on your photo editing journey!

Chapter 12: Advanced Color Adjustments in Adobe Lightroom

In the previous chapter, you mastered advanced photo retouching techniques in Adobe Lightroom. Now, let's delve into the world of advanced color adjustments, where you'll have the power to fine-tune colors, create unique looks, and achieve your desired artistic vision. In this tutorial, you'll learn how to take control of colors in your images and add a personal touch to your photography. Let's get started on your color journey!

Step 1: The Vibrance and Saturation Sliders

In the "Develop" module, locate the "Basic" panel on the right side of the screen.

The "Vibrance" and "Saturation" sliders allow you to adjust the intensity of colors in your image.

Step 2: Understanding Vibrance

The "Vibrance" slider enhances or reduces the intensity of muted colors without overly saturating already vibrant ones.

Increase the slider to make colors more vivid, and decrease it for a more subdued look.

Step 3: Working with Saturation

The "Saturation" slider adjusts the intensity of all colors in your image, regardless of their initial saturation level.

Use this slider with caution, as excessive saturation can result in unnatural-looking images.

Step 4: Fine-Tuning Colors with HSL

The "HSL/Color" panel provides powerful tools for controlling individual colors in your image.

HSL stands for Hue, Saturation, and Luminance, and it allows you to make precise adjustments to specific colors.

Step 5: Adjusting Hue

The "Hue" sliders allow you to shift the color tones of specific ranges in your image.

Experiment with subtle shifts to create different moods and artistic effects.

Step 6: Controlling Saturation

Use the "Saturation" sliders in the "HSL/Color" panel to adjust the intensity of individual colors.

Increase or decrease saturation to make colors pop or blend more harmoniously.

Step 7: Tweaking Luminance

The "Luminance" sliders control the brightness of individual colors in your image.

Adjust luminance to make specific colors brighter or darker, highlighting or subduing certain elements.

Step 8: Creating Split Toning Effects (Optional)

The "Split Toning" panel allows you to add subtle color tints to the highlights and shadows of your image.

Choose complementary colors for a harmonious effect or contrasting colors for a creative look.

Step 9: Utilizing the Tone Curve for Color Control

In addition to tonal adjustments, you can also fine-tune colors using the "Tone Curve" panel.

Create targeted color adjustments by adjusting the red, green, or blue channels in the tone curve.

Step 10: Applying Color Presets (Optional)

To save time and explore different color styles, consider using color presets available in Lightroom.

Browse through the presets in the "Presets" panel to find those that align with your creative vision.

Step 11: Review and Fine-Tuning

Zoom in on your image to review the color adjustments and ensure a cohesive look.

Fine-tune your adjustments to achieve the desired color balance and visual impact.

Step 12: Saving and Exporting

Once you're satisfied with your color adjustments, save your edits by clicking "Done" or "Close" in the "Develop" module.

To export your photo, go to the "File" menu, select "Export," and choose your preferred settings for sharing or printing.

Congratulations! You've now mastered advanced color adjustments in Adobe Lightroom. These techniques will allow you to create captivating images with your unique artistic touch. In the next chapter, we'll explore the world of creative filters and effects, enabling you to add special touches and artistic enhancements to your photos. Keep up the fantastic work on your photo editing journey!

Chapter 13: Creative Filters and Artistic Effects in Adobe Lightroom

In the previous chapter, you explored advanced color adjustments in Adobe Lightroom. Now, let's dive into the realm of creative filters and artistic effects, where you can add special touches and unique enhancements to your photos. In this tutorial, you'll discover how to use Lightroom's creative tools to unleash your creativity and give your images a distinctive look. Let's embark on the journey of artistic expression!

Step 1: Accessing the Effects Panel

Enter the "Develop" module and find the "Effects" panel on the right side of the screen.

The "Effects" panel houses creative tools to apply vignettes, grain, and post-crop vignettes.

Step 2: Adding a Vignette

A vignette darkens or brightens the edges of your image, drawing the viewer's attention toward the center.

In the "Effects" panel, adjust the "Amount" slider to control the strength of the vignette.

Use the "Midpoint" slider to control how far the vignette extends toward the center.

Step 3: Enhancing Grain (Optional)

To create a classic film-like effect, you can add grain to your image using the "Effects" panel.

Increase the "Amount" slider to add more grain, and adjust the "Size" and "Roughness" sliders for the desired texture.

Step 4: Applying Post-Crop Vignetting

If you've already cropped your image, you can apply a post-crop vignette to target the new framing.

In the "Effects" panel, use the "Style" dropdown menu to choose from various vignette styles.

Adjust the "Amount," "Midpoint," "Roundness," and "Feather" sliders to fine-tune the post-crop vignette.

Step 5: Exploring Presets for Creative Effects

Lightroom offers a variety of creative presets that can instantly transform your photos.

In the "Presets" panel, explore categories like "Creative," "Artistic," or "Special Effects" to find presets that suit your vision.

Step 6: Customizing Presets (Optional)

After applying a preset, you can further customize its effects to match your preferences.

Use the sliders in the "Basic," "Tone Curve," and "HSL/Color" panels to fine-tune the preset's impact.

Step 7: Using Split Toning for Creative Tints

Revisit the "Split Toning" panel to add creative color tints to your images.

Experiment with different color combinations to evoke specific moods and atmospheres.

Step 8: Applying Gradient and Radial Filters

The "Graduated Filter" and "Radial Filter" tools can add localized adjustments and creative effects to your photos.

Use the Graduated Filter for gradient adjustments and the Radial Filter for circular adjustments.

Step 9: Creating Dreamy Looks with Soft Focus (Optional)

The "Clarity" slider in the "Basic" panel can be used creatively to create a soft focus or dreamy effect.

Reduce clarity to add a gentle, soft appearance to your image.

Step 10: Review and Fine-Tuning

Zoom in on your image to review the creative filters and effects you've applied.

Fine-tune the adjustments to achieve the artistic look you envision.

Step 11: Saving and Exporting

Once you're satisfied with your creative enhancements, save your edits by clicking "Done" or "Close" in the "Develop" module.

To export your photo, go to the "File" menu, select "Export," and choose your preferred settings for sharing or printing.

Congratulations! You've now mastered creative filters and artistic effects in Adobe Lightroom. These tools empower you to infuse your images with your unique vision and creative flair. In the next chapter, we'll explore the power of local adjustments, enabling you to make precise edits to specific areas in your photos. Keep up the great work on your photo editing journey!

Chapter 14: Mastering Local Adjustments in Adobe Lightroom

In the previous chapter, you explored creative filters and artistic effects in Adobe Lightroom. Now, let's dive deeper into the world of local adjustments, where you'll have the power to make precise edits to specific areas in your photos. In this tutorial, you'll discover how to use Lightroom's local adjustment tools to enhance details, fix imperfections, and draw attention to specific elements. Let's unleash the full potential of your images with masterful local adjustments!

Step 1: The Adjustment Brush

Enter the "Develop" module and find the "Adjustment Brush" tool in the toolbar, or press "K" on your keyboard to activate it.

The Adjustment Brush allows you to paint adjustments onto specific areas in your image.

Step 2: Selecting and Adjusting Brush Settings

Before painting adjustments, set the brush size, feathering, and flow using the sliders or bracket keys "[" and "]".

Adjust the brush settings such as exposure, contrast, clarity, saturation, and more to suit your editing needs.

Step 3: Painting Adjustments

Click and drag with the Adjustment Brush to paint over the area you want to adjust.

The area you paint will be affected by the adjustments you set in the previous step.

Step 4: Erasing and Fine-Tuning

If you make a mistake or need to remove adjustments, switch to the "Eraser" mode by clicking the brush icon with a minus sign (-) or press "Alt" on your keyboard.

Erase adjustments from areas you don't want to be affected.

Use the "O" key to toggle the mask overlay, making it easier to see the areas you've painted.

Step 5: Using the Graduated and Radial Filters

The "Graduated Filter" and "Radial Filter" tools are also local adjustments that create gradient and circular effects, respectively.

Access these tools from the toolbar or press "M" for the Graduated Filter and "Shift + M" for the Radial Filter.

Adjust the settings for exposure, contrast, and other adjustments, and then click and drag to apply the filter.

Step 6: Adding Depth with Radial Filters

The Radial Filter is excellent for adding depth to your images by darkening or brightening the edges.

Create a vignette effect or draw attention to a specific subject with the Radial Filter.

Step 7: Making Precise Adjustments with the Range Mask (Optional)

For more precise local adjustments, utilize the "Range Mask" feature in the "Adjustment Brush" or "Graduated Filter."

The Range Mask allows you to limit adjustments to specific tones, colors, or even luminance in your image.

Step 8: Combining Multiple Local Adjustments

You can apply multiple local adjustments to different areas of your image.

Use the Adjustment Brush, Graduated Filter, and Radial Filter in combination to create complex edits.

Step 9: Review and Fine-Tuning

Zoom in on your image to review the local adjustments and ensure they blend naturally with the overall look.

Fine-tune the adjustments as needed to achieve the desired impact.

Step 10: Saving and Exporting

Once you're satisfied with your local adjustments, save your edits by clicking "Done" or "Close" in the "Develop" module.

To export your photo, go to the "File" menu, select "Export," and choose your preferred settings for sharing or printing.

Congratulations! You've now mastered local adjustments in Adobe Lightroom. These powerful tools give you precise control over your edits and allow you to create stunning, customized images. In the next chapter, we'll explore the art of creating captivating photo collages and stunning panoramas, expanding your creative possibilities even further. Keep up the fantastic work on your photo editing journey!

Chapter 15: Creating Captivating Photo Collages and Stunning Panoramas in Adobe Lightroom

In the previous chapter, you mastered local adjustments in Adobe Lightroom. Now, let's explore the art of creating captivating photo collages and stunning panoramas, expanding your creative possibilities even further. In this tutorial, you'll discover how to combine multiple images into beautiful collages and seamlessly stitch together panoramas for breathtaking results. Let's dive into the world of visual storytelling!

Part 1: Creating Photo Collages

Step 1: Importing Images

Open Adobe Lightroom and import the images you want to use in your collage.

Select the images from the Library module, right-click, and choose "Open as Layers in Photoshop."

Step 2: Sending Images to Photoshop

Lightroom will open Photoshop and automatically load the selected images as layers in a single document.

In Photoshop, arrange and resize the layers to create your desired collage composition.

Step 3: Arranging and Blending Images

Experiment with different layer blending modes, opacity, and layer masks to blend the images seamlessly.

Use tools like the Move Tool (V) and Free Transform (Ctrl/Cmd + T) to position and resize the layers.

Step 4: Adding Creative Elements (Optional)

Incorporate text, graphics, or other design elements to enhance your collage's visual impact.

Utilize Photoshop's creative tools to add your artistic touch to the collage.

Step 5: Saving and Returning to Lightroom

Once you're satisfied with your collage, save the file in Photoshop.

The saved file will automatically appear as a new image in Lightroom.

Step 6: Final Adjustments in Lightroom

In Lightroom, apply any final adjustments or color tweaks to your collage using the Develop module.

Fine-tune the overall look to achieve the desired visual harmony.

Step 7: Saving and Exporting

Save your edits in Lightroom by clicking "Done" or "Close" in the Develop module.

To export your collage, go to the "File" menu, select "Export," and choose your preferred settings for sharing or printing.

Part 2: Creating Stunning Panoramas

Step 1: Importing and Selecting Images

Open Adobe Lightroom and import the images you want to stitch together for your panorama.

Select the images from the Library module, right-click, and choose "Photo Merge" > "Panorama."

Step 2: Photo Merge Options

Lightroom will present the "Panorama Merge Preview" dialog.

Choose the projection type (Spherical, Cylindrical, or Perspective) that best suits your images.

Check the "Auto Crop" box to automatically crop the panorama for a clean result.

Step 3: Merging and Stitching

Click "Merge" to create the panorama.

Lightroom will process and stitch the images together to form the panorama.

Step 4: Cropping and Fine-Tuning

After the merge, use the Crop Tool (R) to adjust the framing of the panorama.

Make any necessary adjustments in the Develop module to enhance the panorama's visual appeal.

Step 5: Additional Adjustments (Optional)

For further refinements, use the local adjustment tools, such as the Graduated Filter or Adjustment Brush, to make targeted adjustments to specific areas.

Fine-tune the overall colors and tones to achieve the desired effect.

Step 6: Saving and Exporting

Save your edits in Lightroom by clicking "Done" or "Close" in the Develop module.

To export your panorama, go to the "File" menu, select "Export," and choose your preferred settings for sharing or printing.

Congratulations! You've now mastered the art of creating captivating photo collages and stunning panoramas in Adobe Lightroom. These techniques allow you to unleash your creativity and tell visual stories with your images. With your newfound skills, you can take your photo editing journey to new heights. Keep experimenting, learning, and pushing the boundaries of your artistic expression. Happy editing!

Chapter 16: Printing and Publishing Your Masterpieces from Adobe Lightroom

In the previous chapter, you learned how to create captivating photo collages and stunning panoramas in Adobe Lightroom. Now, let's explore the final steps of your photo editing journey, where you'll discover how to showcase your masterpieces to the world. In this tutorial, you'll learn how to prepare your images for printing and publishing, ensuring they look their best in various formats. Let's get ready to share your creativity with the world!

Part 1: Preparing for Printing

Step 1: Calibrating Your Monitor (Optional but Recommended)

For accurate color representation, consider calibrating your monitor using a hardware calibrator.

Calibrating your monitor ensures that what you see on the screen matches the printed output.

Step 2: Image Sizing and Resolution

Decide on the size and resolution of your printed image.

For most prints, a resolution of 300 pixels per inch (PPI) is ideal, but check with your printer for their recommended resolution.

Step 3: Soft Proofing (Optional)

Use Lightroom's soft proofing feature to simulate how your image will appear when printed.

Go to the "Develop" module, select "Soft Proofing" from the toolbar, and choose your printer's ICC profile.

Step 4: Adjusting for Printing

Make any necessary adjustments to your image for printing, such as sharpening and color corrections.

Use the "Detail" panel to apply output sharpening specific to the print size and medium.

Step 5: Cropping for Printing

If needed, use the Crop Tool (R) to ensure your image fits the desired print aspect ratio.

Pay attention to the composition and ensure nothing essential gets cut off.

Step 6: Exporting for Printing

Go to the "File" menu and choose "Export."

Select your preferred file format (JPEG or TIFF) and the destination folder for the printed images.

Adjust the quality settings and image size based on your printing requirements.

Step 7: Printing Test Proofs (Optional)

Before printing large quantities, consider printing test proofs to evaluate the colors and quality.

Make any final adjustments if necessary before printing the final version.

Part 2: Preparing for Publishing

Step 1: Image Sizing and Resolution for Web

For web publishing, resize your images to the appropriate dimensions and resolution (usually 72 PPI).

Use the Export function in Lightroom to save your images for the web.

Step 2: Watermarking (Optional)

To protect your images when sharing online, consider adding a watermark.

Create a watermark in Lightroom's "Watermark Editor" and apply it during export.

Step 3: Choosing the Right File Format

For web publishing, JPEG is the most common file format, providing a good balance of quality and file size.

Use the Export function to save your images as JPEGs with the desired quality settings.

Step 4: Exporting for Social Media and Websites

Go to the "File" menu and choose "Export."

Select the JPEG file format, adjust the quality settings, and choose the destination folder for the web-ready images.

Step 5: Sharing on Social Media and Websites

Upload your images to social media platforms or your website to showcase your work to a broader audience.

Share your images with appropriate captions and tags to engage your audience.

Congratulations! You've now learned how to prepare your images for printing and publishing in Adobe Lightroom. Whether displaying your masterpieces in print or sharing them online, these techniques ensure your images look their best in any format. With your creative journey complete, don't stop exploring, experimenting, and growing as a photographer and photo editor. The possibilities are endless, and your artistic vision knows no bounds. Keep creating, sharing, and inspiring others with your passion for photography!

Chapter 17: Efficient Workflow Tips and Time-Saving Techniques in Adobe Lightroom

In the previous chapter, you learned how to prepare your images for printing and publishing in Adobe Lightroom. Now, let's explore efficient workflow tips and time-saving techniques to streamline your photo editing process and maximize productivity. In this tutorial, you'll discover essential shortcuts, organization methods, and automation tools that will help you work smarter and faster in Lightroom. Let's optimize your workflow for a seamless editing experience!

Step 1: Importing and Organizing

Utilizing Import Presets:

Create import presets with your preferred settings, such as metadata, keywords, and develop settings.

Apply these presets upon import to save time and maintain consistency across your images.

Smart Folders and Collections:

Organize your images using Smart Folders based on specific criteria like date, rating, or keywords.

Utilize Collections to group related images for easier access during editing.

Step 2: Keyboard Shortcuts and Tools

Mastering Keyboard Shortcuts:

Learn and utilize essential keyboard shortcuts in Lightroom for common tasks.

Memorize shortcuts for Library, Develop, and Export modules to speed up your workflow.

Customizing the Toolbar:

Customize the Develop module's toolbar to include your most frequently used tools.

Right-click on the toolbar and select "Customize Toolbar" to add or remove tools for quick access.

Sync and Auto-Sync:

Use the "Sync" and "Auto-Sync" features to apply the same adjustments to multiple images simultaneously.

Select the source image, apply adjustments, then sync with other selected images or enable Auto-Sync.

Step 3: Virtual Copies and Snapshots

Creating Virtual Copies:

Use Virtual Copies to create different versions of an image with various edits.

Experiment with different editing styles without creating duplicate files.

Snapshots for Editing Stages:

Take Snapshots during your editing process to save different stages of adjustments.

Easily compare and revert to previous editing versions as needed.

Step 4: Using Presets and Templates

Customizing Develop Presets:

Create your own Develop presets for frequently used
adjustments or your signature editing style.

Apply these presets to individual or multiple images for a
consistent look.

Utilizing Export Presets:

Save Export presets with your preferred settings for various
output sizes and formats.

Streamline the exporting process and ensure optimal results.

Step 5: GPU Acceleration and Performance

Enabling GPU Acceleration:

In Lightroom's Preferences, enable GPU acceleration to leverage your graphics card's power for faster image processing.

Note that not all systems support GPU acceleration.

Smart Previews for Improved Performance:

Generate Smart Previews for faster editing, especially when working with large RAW files or on slower systems.

Smart Previews allow you to edit offline or on a laptop without accessing the original files.

Step 6: Backing Up and Syncing

Regular Backups:

Create regular backups of your Lightroom catalog to safeguard your work.

Schedule automated backups or manually create backups from the Catalog Settings.

Utilizing Lightroom Cloud Sync (Optional):

If you use Lightroom cloud storage, take advantage of the sync feature to access your images and edits across devices.

Enable Lightroom sync in the Preferences to sync your catalog and collections.

Congratulations! You've now learned efficient workflow tips and time-saving techniques in Adobe Lightroom. These practices will boost your productivity, allowing you to focus on your creative process and create exceptional images. As you continue your photo editing journey, remember to stay organized, experiment with new tools, and embrace continuous learning. With an optimized workflow, your editing prowess will soar, and your photography will reach new heights. Happy editing!

Chapter 18: Advanced Editing Techniques in Adobe Lightroom

In the previous chapter, you explored efficient workflow tips and time-saving techniques in Adobe Lightroom. Now, let's take your editing skills to the next level with advanced techniques to bring out the best in your images. In this tutorial, you'll discover powerful tools and adjustments that can elevate your photos to new heights. Let's dive into the world of advanced editing in Lightroom!

Step 1: Mastering Graduated and Radial Filters

Fine-Tuning Graduated Filters:

Use the Graduated Filter to balance exposure in challenging lighting conditions.

Adjust exposure, highlights, shadows, and other settings to seamlessly blend the filtered area with the rest of the image.

Creating Artistic Effects with Radial Filters:

The Radial Filter is not only for basic adjustments; it can add creative effects too.

Experiment with exposure, clarity, and other settings to draw attention to your subject or add vignettes.

Step 2: Advanced Tone Curve Adjustments

Fine Control with Parametric Curve:

Master the Parametric Tone Curve for precise control over highlights, shadows, and midtones.

Create custom S-shaped curves for unique tonal adjustments.

Targeted Adjustments with Point Curve:

Switch to the Point Curve to make targeted adjustments by clicking and dragging on the curve.

Adjust specific tonal ranges or colors for a tailored look.

Step 3: Correcting Perspective Distortions

Using the Guided Upright Tool:

Correct perspective distortions and converging lines with the Guided Upright Tool.

Draw vertical and horizontal lines on your image to align elements accurately.

Manual Transform Adjustments:

For more complex distortions, use the Transform panel's manual adjustments.

Fine-tune vertical, horizontal, and aspect transformations to achieve the desired perspective correction.

Step 4: Creative Editing with Camera Profiles

Exploring Camera Profiles:

Experiment with different Camera Profiles to change the look and color rendering of your images.

Profiles offer distinct styles that can set the mood and atmosphere of your photos.

Custom Camera Profiles (Optional):

Create custom Camera Profiles using the X-Rite ColorChecker Passport or other calibration tools.

This advanced technique ensures color accuracy and consistency across different lighting conditions.

Step 5: Working with Advanced Brushes

Refining Adjustment Brushes:

Utilize the Adjustment Brush to apply targeted adjustments to specific areas of your image.

Use the new Range Mask options to further refine your adjustments.

Advanced Healing and Cloning:

Combine the Spot Removal Tool with the Clone and Heal options to tackle more complex retouching tasks.

Remove distracting elements or imperfections with precision.

Step 6: Creating Panoramic HDR Images (Optional)

Merging Panoramas:

Use the Merge feature to create panoramic images from multiple overlapping shots.

Select your images, go to the "Photo" menu, and choose "Photo Merge" > "Panorama."

Combining HDR and Panoramas:

For challenging lighting situations, consider creating HDR panoramas.

Capture bracketed exposures, merge them into HDR images, and then merge those images into a panorama.

Step 7: Creating Stunning Monochromes

Mastering Black and White Mix:

Fine-tune the Black & White Mix sliders to control the luminance of individual colors in your black and white images.

Adjust the sliders to achieve the desired tonal contrast and mood.

Creative Toning:

Experiment with Split Toning to add subtle color toning to your monochrome images.

Choose hues for highlights and shadows to give your images a unique look.

Congratulations! You've now learned advanced editing techniques in Adobe Lightroom. These powerful tools and adjustments will empower you to create breathtaking images and express your unique artistic vision. As you continue to refine your editing skills, remember to experiment, explore new possibilities, and push the boundaries of your creativity. Keep honing your craft, and your photography will continue to evolve and amaze. Happy editing!

Chapter 19: Preserving and Restoring Old Photos in Adobe Lightroom

In this chapter, we'll explore a special skill set – preserving and restoring old photos in Adobe Lightroom. Whether you've inherited family photographs or discovered old prints, these techniques will help you revive cherished memories and preserve precious moments for generations to come. Let's dive into the art of restoring and enhancing vintage images!

Step 1: Scanning Old Photos

Use a High-Quality Scanner:

To preserve image quality, use a high-resolution flatbed scanner for scanning prints.

Set the resolution to at least 300 PPI for standard prints, and higher for smaller images or detailed shots.

Dust and Clean the Photos:

Before scanning, ensure photos are free from dust and debris.

Use an anti-static brush or compressed air to clean the photos gently.

Step 2: Importing and Organizing Old Photos

Create a Dedicated Folder:

Organize your scanned images into a separate folder or subfolder within your Lightroom catalog.

Create a meaningful naming convention to identify the images easily.

Utilize Keywords:

Add relevant keywords to your old photos for easy searching and sorting.

Include names of individuals, locations, and significant events.

Step 3: Restoring and Enhancing Old Photos

Use the Basic Panel:

Start with the Basic panel to adjust exposure, contrast, highlights, and shadows.

Make adjustments to improve the overall tonal range of the image.

Graduated Filters for Vignettes:

Use the Graduated Filter to create a gentle vignette effect around the edges of the photo.

This can help draw attention to the central subject and improve the overall composition.

Spot Removal for Dust and Scratches:

Utilize the Spot Removal tool to remove dust spots, scratches, and minor blemishes.

Set the tool to Heal or Clone mode, depending on the type of correction required.

Adjustment Brush for Local Corrections:

Apply targeted adjustments using the Adjustment Brush to specific areas that need attention.

Use the brush to brighten faces, enhance eyes, or add subtle sharpening to important elements.

Step 4: Cropping and Straightening

Crop for Composition:

Use the Crop Tool to improve the composition of your old photos.

Remove distracting elements and focus on the main subject.

Straighten Horizons:

Correct any tilted horizons using the Straighten Tool or the Angle slider in the Crop panel.

Ensure the horizon is level and the image is well-balanced.

Step 5: Color Correction (Optional)

Utilize the Color Panel:

If your old photos have color shifts or fading, use the Color panel to correct white balance and color tones.

Adjust temperature, tint, and individual color sliders as needed.

Enhance with Split Toning (Optional):

Add subtle color toning to black and white images using the Split Toning panel.

Experiment with hues for highlights and shadows to create a vintage or artistic look.

Step 6: Review and Fine-Tuning

Zoom in for Details:

Carefully inspect your restored image at 100% magnification to catch any missed imperfections.

Look for artifacts, noise, or areas that need additional retouching.

Compare with Original:

Use the "Before and After" view or the "Y" key to compare your edited photo with the original scan.

Ensure your edits have improved the image without overdoing it.

Step 7: Saving and Exporting

Save Your Restored Image:

Save your edits in Lightroom by clicking "Done" or "Close" in the Develop module.

Your restored image is now safely stored in your Lightroom catalog.

Export for Printing or Sharing:

To print or share your restored photo, go to the "File" menu, select "Export," and choose your preferred settings.

Save the file as a high-quality JPEG or TIFF for printing or digital sharing.

Congratulations! You've now learned how to preserve and restore old photos in Adobe Lightroom. These skills will enable you to breathe new life into cherished memories and ensure they stand the test of time. As you continue restoring old photos, remember to approach the process with care and patience. Each image holds a unique story, and your skilled editing will preserve these memories for generations to come. Happy restoring!

Chapter 20: Printing Fine Art and Creating Photo Books in Adobe Lightroom

In this final chapter, we'll explore two exciting ways to showcase your photography – printing fine art and creating photo books in Adobe Lightroom. These methods allow you to transform your digital images into tangible, beautiful creations that you can hold and display with pride. Let's dive into the world of fine art printing and photo book creation!

Part 1: Printing Fine Art

Step 1: Preparing Your Image for Printing

Review Image Quality:

Before printing, ensure your image meets the necessary resolution and quality requirements.

Verify that the image size matches the desired print dimensions.

Soft Proofing for Print:

Enable Soft Proofing in the Develop module to preview how your image will appear in print.

Select the ICC profile of your printer and paper combination to simulate the print output.

Step 2: Choosing the Right Paper and Printer

Selecting Fine Art Paper:

Choose a high-quality fine art paper that complements the characteristics of your image.

Consider factors such as surface texture, weight, and archival properties.

Printing at Home or Using a Professional Printer:

Decide whether to print at home if you have a high-quality printer or use a professional print service.

Professional printers often offer a wide range of paper options and produce exceptional results.

Step 3: Printing Your Image

Printer Settings:

Ensure you select the appropriate printer settings, such as paper type and print quality.

Choose the correct color management options to maintain color accuracy.

Test Printing:

Perform a test print on the chosen paper to verify color accuracy and quality.

Adjust any necessary settings before printing the final image.

Step 4: Handling and Framing Your Print

Properly Handling Prints:

Handle your fine art print with care to avoid fingerprints, smudges, or damage.

Wear clean, lint-free gloves when handling the print.

Framing and Displaying:

Choose a high-quality frame and mat that complements your print.

Display your print in a location with proper lighting and minimal exposure to direct sunlight.

Part 2: Creating Photo Books

Step 1: Selecting Your Images

Curate Your Collection:

Choose a selection of images that tell a cohesive story or represent a particular theme.

Ensure the images flow smoothly when presented together.

Organizing Your Layout:

Create a virtual folder or collection for the images you plan to include in your photo book.

Arrange the images in the desired sequence to build your narrative.

Step 2: Designing Your Photo Book

Using the Book Module:

Enter the Book module in Lightroom to start designing your photo book.

Select the book format, size, and cover type.

Customizing Page Layouts:

Customize your photo book's page layouts using the drag-and-drop interface.

Experiment with different image placements and text options.

Step 3: Adding Captions and Text

Including Captions and Descriptions:

Add captions and descriptions to your images to provide context and enhance the storytelling.

Use the Text panel to add text boxes with relevant information.

Selecting Fonts and Styles:

Choose fonts and styles that complement the theme and tone of your photo book.

Ensure readability and consistency throughout the book.

Step 4: Previewing and Ordering Your Photo Book

Previewing Your Photo Book:

Before ordering, use the Book module's preview option to review the layout and content.

Check for any errors or design issues.

Ordering Your Photo Book:

Once you're satisfied with the layout, click the "Order Book" button in the Book module.

Select your preferred print provider and options for size, cover, and paper type.

Congratulations! You've now learned how to print fine art and create photo books in Adobe Lightroom. These methods allow you to share your photography in tangible forms and enjoy your work beyond the digital screen. Whether you're printing fine art for display or creating photo books as cherished keepsakes, these techniques will elevate your photography to new heights. Embrace the joy of holding your images in your hands and sharing them with others. Keep honing your skills, exploring new possibilities, and capturing beautiful moments through your lens. Happy printing and book designing!

www.ingramcontent.com/pod-product-compliance
Lightning Source LLC
LaVergne TN
LVHW051713050326
832903LV00032B/4184